60+ Most Popular Patterns

Chart
Patterns
Trading-Desk Booklet

Satish Gaire

ISBN-13: 978-1-951403-04-1 (Paperback)
ISBN-13: 978-1-951403-05-8 (eBook)

The authors disclaim responsibility for adverse effects or consequences form the misapplication or injudicious use of the information contained in this book. Mention of resources and associations does not imply an endorsement.

Chapter Organization *by* Nikesh Chapagain
Book Organizer *by* Lexin Huo
Book Interior *by* Pankaj Runthala
Book Cover *by* Casey Fritz
Gratitude *to* Rajan Pandey

First Edition

"Stock Market is a vehicle that can have astounding impact on your life, Let's make that a *positive* one."

Labor Omnia Vincit

Unlock Extra Tools & Resources
EvilTrader.net

Disclaimer

The author and EvilTrader.net ("the company"), including its employees, contractors, shareholders and affiliates, is NOT investment advisory service. We are not registered as a securities broker-dealer or an investment adviser either with the U.S. Securities and Exchange Commission (the "SEC") or with any state securities regulatory authority. We are neither licensed nor qualified to provide investment advice. To the fullest extent of the law, we will not be liable to any person or entity for the quality, accuracy, completeness, reliability, or timeliness of the information provided in the report, or for any direct, indirect, consequential, incidental, special or punitive damages that may arise out of the use of information we provide to any person or entity (including, but not limited to, lost profits, loss of opportunities, trading losses, and damages that may result from any inaccuracy or incompleteness of this information). Every trade you make is your own trade and you are fully responsible for any gain or loss you shall incur. EvilTrader.net, nor any moderators are held liable for any losses you shall have at any time you are with our service or after. It should be not be assumed that the methods, techniques or indicators provided in the book will be profitable nor that they will not result in loss. All information is provided for educational purpose only. Investors and traders must always consult with their licensed advisors or tax advisors to determine the suitability of any investment. We are not liable for any consequences that may occur by using information on this book.

How To Use This Book

Glad you asked! Let's be honest, No-one can predict what's going to happen in the stock market with 100% certainty, but we can get close...

Whenever you see that small candle stick on your trading software, that was made possible by millions of people around the globe reacting to two emotions: greed & fear. Millions of "Homo-sapiens" who think they have conquered the world, but in fact, we are nothing more than Monkeys with some plans. No matter how advance we get, human behavior hasn't changed for decades & probably won't for awhile & that's a good thing for you.

Chart Patterns are nothing more than reflection of human behavior in massive scale & the best part is that it's predictable (most of the time).

2 Ways To Use This Book To Make You Better Trader:

- ✓ Keep It Next To Your Trading Desk
- ✓ Flip Through It Once A Week

This booklet is going to serve you for years to come!

Chart Patterns Index

Chart Patterns Index

Chart Patterns : Trading-Desk Booklet | Satish Gaire

Chart Patterns Index

Chart Patterns Index

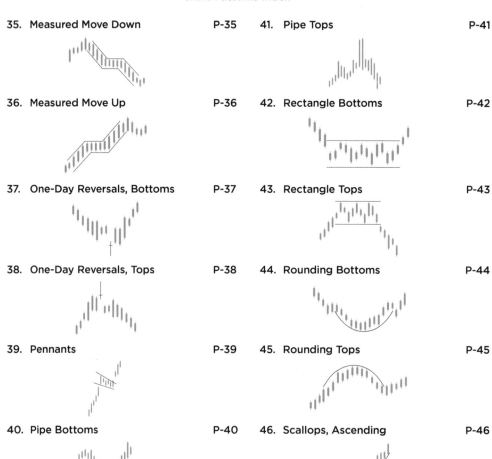

Chart Patterns : Trading-Desk Booklet | Satish Gaire

Chart Patterns Index

Chart Patterns : Trading-Desk Booklet | Satish Gaire

Chart Patterns Index

59. Wedges, Rising

P-59

60. Weekly Reversals, Downside

P-60

61. Weekly Reversals, Upside

P-61

1 Broadening Bottoms

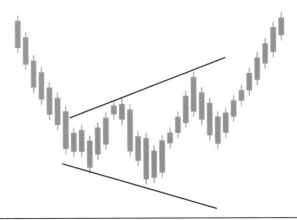

Characteristic	Discussion
Price trend	Downward leading to the pattern.
Shape	Higher peaks and lower valleys. Megaphone Shape
Trendlines	The top trend line slopes upward, the bottom one slopes downward.
Touches	At least five touches total, three peaks or three valleys should touch the associated trend line with two or more touches of the other trendline.
White space	Price should cross the pattern from side to side, filling the area with price movement.
Volume	Upward 65% (up breakouts) to 67% (down breakouts) of the time.
Breakout	It could occur in any direction (upward 60% of the time) and it happens when price pierces a trendline or moves above/below the end of the pattern.

2 Broadening Formations

Right-Angled and Ascending

Characteristic	Discussion
Price trend	Can be up (74% have a rising price trend) leading to the pattern.
Shape	A megaphone tilted up with the bottom horizontal.
Trendlines	The bottom trendline is horizontal, the top one slopes upward.
Touches	At least five touches total, three peaks or three valleys should touch the associated trend line with two or more touches of the other trendline. Ideally, the second of three touches will touch (instead of coming 'close' to) the trendline.
Volume	Trends upward 62% to 63% of the time.
Breakout	Upward 55% of the time.

Satish Gaire

3 Broadening Formations
Right-Angled and Descending

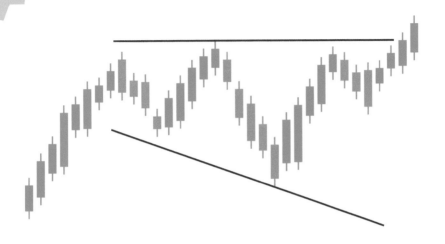

Characteristic	Discussion
Price trend	Can be up or down leading to the pattern.
Shape	A megaphone tilted down with the top horizontal.
Trendlines	The top trendline is horizontal, the bottom one slopes downward.
Touches	At least five touches total, three peaks or three valleys should touch the associated trend line with two or more touches of the other trendline. Ideally, the second of three touches will touch (instead of coming 'close' to) the trendline.
Breakout	Upward 64% of the time.

4 Broadening Tops

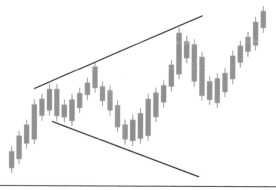

Characteristic	Discussion
Price trend	Upward leading to the pattern. That is, the trend start is below the pattern's start.
Shape	Higher peaks and lower valleys -- a megaphone shape.
Trendlines	The top trendline slopes upward, the bottom one slopes downward.
Touches	At least five touches total, three peaks or three valleys should touch the associated trend line with two or more touches of the other trendline. Ideally, the second of three touches will touch (instead of coming 'close' to) the trendline. This avoids the identification problem where price forms an up-sloping channel with an upward spike at pattern's end.
White space	Price should cross the pattern from side to side, filling the area with price movement.
Breakout	Can occur in any direction (upward 60%) and it happens when price pierces a trendline or moves above/below the end of the pattern.

Satish Gaire

5 Broadening Wedges

Ascending

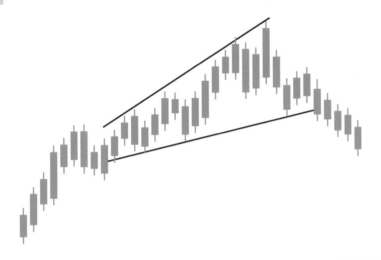

Characteristic	Discussion
Price trend	Can be up or down leading to the pattern
Shape	A megaphone tilted up. Refer to the above figure.
Trendlines	Both trendlines slope upward. The top one slopes more steeply than the bottom one.
Touches	At least three peaks and three valleys should touch their respective trendline.
Volume	Irregular but trends upward 66% to 67% of the time.
Breakout	Downward 52% of the time.

6 **Broadening Wedges**

Descending

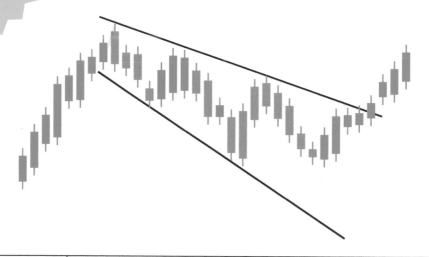

Characteristic	Discussion
Price trend	Can be up or down leading to the pattern.
Shape	A megaphone tilted down.
Trendlines	Both trendlines slope downward.
Touches	For proper identification, look for at least five trendline touches (three or more touches of one trendline, two or more of the other) at minor highs or lows. Price cutting through a trendline doesn't count as a touch (that happens most at the start and breakout of the pattern).
Volume trend	Trends upward.

Satish Gaire

7 Bump-and-Run
Reversal Bottoms

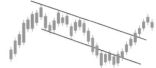

Characteristic	Discussion
Shape	A frying pan, tilted down, with the handle on the left.
Trendline	During the beginning of the pattern, price often follows a down-sloping trendline that ranges from 0 to 45 degrees (rarely more).
Lead-in phase	The handle portion of the frying pan is called the lead-in phase as it leads in to the bump phase. The chart to the lower right shows the location.
Lead-in height	Measures from the trendline drawn across the highs to the handle low. Select the widest distance between the trendline and the low, measured vertically, in the first quarter of the chart pattern. The chart to the right shows an example. The height is between the two blue dots.
Lead-in duration	At least a month (average is 35 days), but this varies widely.
Bump phase	This is the frying pan. The down-sloping trendline deepens to 60 degrees or more. Price drops rapidly then levels out and turns around, forming a rounded turn. Price may pause at the 0 to 45-degree trendline (see Trendline above) before moving higher. The chart to the right shows the location of the bump phase.
Bump height	Measured from the trendline to the lowest low, vertically, and it should be at least twice the lead-in height (but allow variation). The chart to the right shows the measure between the two blue dots.
Uphill run	After the bump phase, price begins an uphill run. I show the run phase on the chart to the right.
Volume	High during the start of the pattern, the bump start, and upward breakout.
Confirmation	The pattern confirms when price closes above the down-sloping trendline. Do NOT accept any patterns which does not show a close above the blue trendline (after pattern's end).

8 Bump-and-Run
Reversal Tops

Characteristic	Discussion
Rising trendline	A trendline connecting the price valleys rises upward at 30 to 45 degrees, but this varies with scaling. Do not use horizontal or near-horizontal trendlines and avoid patterns with steep (over 60 degrees) trendlines.
Lead-in phase	The lead-in is the section at the start of the pattern and it precedes the bump phase. Price follows a rising trendline. The figure to the lower right shows an example.
Lead-in height	The tallest distance in the first quarter of the chart pattern, measured vertically, is the lead-in height. Must be at least $1, but preferably $2 or more. The chart on the right shows the measure between the two blue dots, vertically, from trendline to price low.
Lead-in duration	At least a month, but be flexible.
Bump phase	Price rises in the bump phase following a steeper trendline (45 to 60 degrees) on high volume usually after a favorable event (earnings report, rating upgrades). Price rounds over and eventually returns to the lower, 30-degree trendline setup in the lead-in phase. The chart on the right shows an example.
Bump height	Measured from the peak to the 30-degree trendline, it should be at least twice the lead-in height (but be flexible). The chart on the right shows an example between the two blue dots.
Downhill run	After price returns to the 30-degree trendline, price may bump up and form additional bumps or slide along the trendline before plunging lower in a downhill run. The figure to the right shows one bump up followed by the downhill run.
Volume	High at the start of the pattern, at the bump start, and at the downward breakout (where price pierces the 30-degree trendline).
Confirmation	The pattern confirms as a valid one when price closes below the 30-degree trendline. If price does not close below the trendline, then you do NOT have a valid pattern.

Satish Gaire

9 Cup with Handle

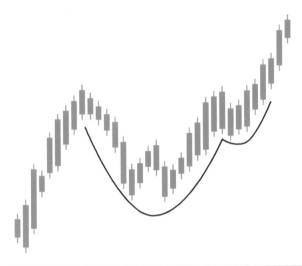

Characteristic	Discussion
Price trend	Price rises into the start of the cup.
Shape	A rounded turn that looks like a cup with a handle on the right.
U-shaped cup	The cup should be U-shaped, not V-shaped.
Handle	The cup must have a handle on the right.
Cup duration	From 7 to 65 weeks
Handle	1 week minimum with no maximum, forming in the upper half of the cup.
Cup	Cup rims should be near the same price level but be flexible.

Cup with Handle

Inverted

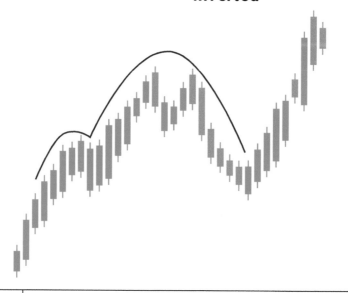

Characteristic	Discussion
Rounded turn	Look for a smooth, rounded looking turn (an inverted cup), but allow exceptions.
Cup rims	The two cup rims should bottom near the same price.
Cup handle	To the right of the cup should be a handle.
Cup retrace	Handle must not rise above the cup top but often retrace 30% to 60% up the height of the cup.
Confirmation	The pattern confirms as a valid one when price clos

Satish Gaire

Dead-Cat Bounce

Characteristic	Discussion
Price gap	Price usually gaps downward, closing 15% to 70% lower than the prior day. The average event decline from prior close to trend low is 31%.
Trend low	Forty-six percent make a lower low the next day, 17% continue lower the next day, then 9%, and then 3%, respectively. From the event day to the trend low averages 7 days.
Bounce	After the event day decline, price bounces. Twenty-two percent will close the gap during the bounce phase, 38% will close it in 3 months, and 58% will close the gap in 6 months. The average bounce height from event low to bounce high is 28% and takes 23 days.
Post bounce decline	Once the bounce completes, price resumes declining, averaging 30% from the bounce high to post bounce low in 49 days. This places price an average of 18% below the event low 67% of the time.
Second dead-cat bounce	Twenty-six percent will have a second dead-cat bounce measuring at least 15% within 3 months, and 38% will dead-cat bounce within 6 months.

12 Dead-Cat Bounce

Inverted

Characteristic	Discussion
Price rise	Look for an event that causes price to jump at least 5% but it can be 20%, 50%, or even higher. Avoid those stocks with takeover rumors as they tend to stay high or move even higher.
Higher high	Price typically moves higher the day following the event.
Decline	After that, price tends to decline.

Satish Gaire

13 Diamond Bottoms

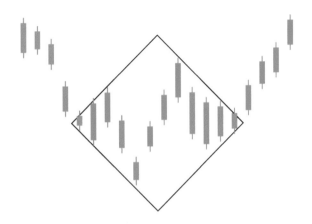

Characteristic	Discussion
Price trend	Downward leading to the pattern.
Shape	Looks like a diamond, but usually one tilted to the side.
Trendlines	Prices form higher peaks and lower valleys in the first part of the pattern, then price action narrows with lower peaks and higher valleys. Trendlines outline many of the peaks and valleys, forming a diamond shape.
Touches	Prices will touch each trendline once or twice. Don't worry if your lines cross some of the price outliers.
Volume trend	Downward trend 67% of the time.
Breakout	Upward 74% of the time, when price closes outside one of the trendline boundaries.

14 Diamond Tops

Characteristic	Discussion
Price trend	Upward leading to the pattern.
Shape	Looks like a diamond, but one usually tilted to the side.
Trendlines	Prices form higher peaks and lower valleys in the first part of the pattern, then price action narrows with lower peaks and higher valleys. Trendlines connect the peaks and valleys for a diamond shape.
Touches	Prices will touch each trendline once or twice. Don't worry if your lines cross some of the price outliers.
Volume trend	Downward trend 55% to 59% of the time.
Breakout	Downward 54% of the time.

Satish Gaire

15 Double Bottoms
Adam & Adam

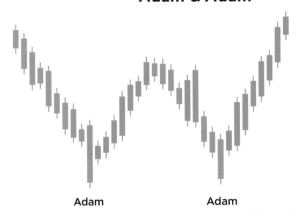

Adam   Adam

Characteristic	Discussion
Price trend	Downward leading to the pattern
Shape	Two distinct valleys that look similar. Adam bottoms are narrow, V-shaped, sometimes with one long price spike.
Peak	The rise between bottoms should measure at least 10%, but allow wide variations.
Bottom price	The price variation between bottoms is small (the average is 1%, but allow variations). The two valleys should appear to bottom near the same price.
Separation	The twin valleys are usually several weeks apart (16 days is the median).
Confirmation	The double bottom confirms as a true double bottom once price closes above the peak between the two valleys.
Volume	Usually higher on formation of the first bottom.

16 Double Bottoms

Adam & Eve

Eve

Adam

Characteristic	Discussion
Price trend	Downward leading to the pattern.
Shape	Two distinct valleys that look different. Adam bottoms appear first and are narrow, V-shaped, sometimes with one long price spike. Eve bottoms appear after Adam and are wide and more rounded looking. Spikes that appear tend to be more numerous and shorter on Eve bottoms.
Peak	The rise between bottoms should measure at least 10%, but allow variations. Tall patterns perform better.
Bottom price	The price variation between bottoms is small. The two valleys should appear to bottom near the same price.
Separation	The average separation between bottoms is almost two months.
Confirmation	The double bottom confirms as a true double bottom once price closes above the peak between the two valleys. See the figure to the right. Without confirmation you do not have an Adam & Eve double bottom, just squiggles on a chart.
Volume	Usually higher on formation of the left valley.

Satish Gaire

Double Bottoms
Eve & Adam

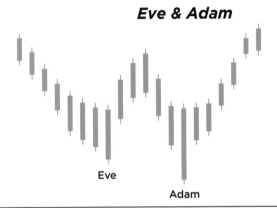

Eve

Adam

Characteristic	Discussion
Price trend	Downward leading to the pattern.
Shape	Two distinct valleys that look different. Eve bottoms appear first and are wider and more rounded looking. Adam bottoms appear after Eve and are narrow, V-shaped, sometimes with one long price spike. Spikes that appear tend to be more numerous and shorter on Eve bottoms.
Peak	The rise between bottoms should measure at least 10%, but allow variations.
Bottom price	The price variation between bottoms is small, usually between 0% and 4%. The two valleys should appear to bottom near the same price.
Separation	The twin valleys are several weeks apart with most falling in the 2 to 7 week range (the median is 23 days).
Confirmation	The double bottom confirms as a true double bottom once price closes above the peak between the two valleys.
Volume	Higher on the left bottom.

18 Double Bottoms
Eve & Eve

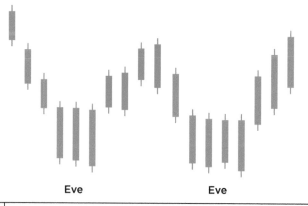

Eve   Eve

Characteristic	Discussion
Price trend	Downward leading to the pattern.
Shape	Two distinct valleys that look similar. Eve bottoms are wide and more rounded appearing. Spikes that appear tend to be numerous and short.
Peak	The rise between bottoms should measure at least 10%, but allow variations.
Bottom price	The price variation between bottoms is small, usually between 0% and 6%. The two valleys should appear to bottom near the same price.
Separation	The twin valleys are several weeks apart with most falling in the 2 to 7 week range.
Confirmation	The double bottom confirms as a true double bottom once price closes above the peak between the two valleys.
Volume	Usually higher on the left bottom.

Satish Gaire

19 Double Tops
Adam & Adam

Adam

Adam

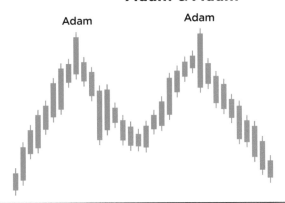

Characteristic	Discussion
Price trend	Upward leading to the pattern.
Shape	Two distinct tops that look similar, usually twin spikes poking above the surrounding price landscape. Adam tops are narrow, inverted V's.
Valley	The valley drop between the tops should measure at least 10%, but allow exceptions.
Top price	The variation between price peaks is small, usually less than 3%. The two tops should appear to peak near the same price.
Separation	The twin peaks are usually several weeks apart.
Confirmation	The double top confirms as a true double top once price closes below the valley between the two peaks.
Volume	Usually higher on formation of the left peak than the right, and trends downward.

Double Tops
Adam & Eve

Characteristic	Discussion
Price trend	Upward leading to the pattern.
Shape	Two distinct tops that look different. Adam tops appear first and are narrow, inverted Vs but Eve follows Adam and is more rounded looking and wider than Adam.
Valley	The valley drop between the tops should measure at least 10%, but allow exceptions.
Top price	The variation between price peaks is small, less than 3%. The two tops should appear to peak near the same price.
Separation	The twin peaks are several weeks apart with most falling in 2 to 7 week range.
Confirmation	The double top confirms as a true double top once price closes below the valley between the two peaks.
Volume	Usually higher on formation of the left peak than the right.

Satish Gaire

Double Tops
Eve & Adam

Characteristic	Discussion
Price trend	Upward leading to the pattern.
Shape	Two distinct tops that look different. Eve appears first and is rounded looking and wider than Adam. Adam comes second and is narrow, an inverted V, often appears as a 1-day price spike.
Valley	The valley drop between the tops should measure at least 10%, but allow exceptions.
Top price	The variation between price peaks is small, often less than 3%. The two tops should appear to peak near the same price.
Separation	The twin peaks are several weeks apart with most falling in the 2 to 6 week range.
Confirmation	The double top confirms as a true double top once price closes below the valley between the two peaks.
Volume	Usually higher on formation of the left peak.

Double Tops

Eve & Eve

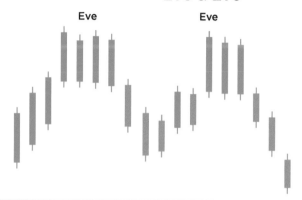

Eve   Eve

Characteristic	Discussion
Price trend	Upward leading to the pattern.
Shape	Two distinct tops that look similar. An Eve top is rounded and wide looking, but sometimes has several short spikes poking out.
Valley	The valley drop between the tops should measure at least 10%, but allow exceptions.
Top price	The variation between price peaks is small, often less than 3%. The two tops should appear to peak near the same price.
Separation	The twin peaks are several weeks apart with most falling in the 2 to 6 week range.
Confirmation	The double top confirms as a true double top once price closes below the valley between the two peaks.
Volume	Usually higher on formation of the left peak.

Satish Gaire

23 Flags

Characteristic	Discussion
Price trend	Can be any direction leading to the chart pattern.
Shape	Looks like a small rectangle often tilted against the prevailing price trend.
Trend lines	Price moves between two parallel, or near parallel, trendlines.
3 weeks	Flags are short, less than 3 weeks long. Patterns longer than that are rectangles or channels.
Flagpole	The flagpole which leads to the flag should be unusually steep and last several days.
Volume trend	Downward trend 74% (up breakouts) to 77% (down breakouts) of the time.
Breakout	Upward 60% of the time.

24

Flags
High and Tight

Characteristic	Discussion
Price trend	Upward leading to the flag. Price must rise at least 90% (shoot for a double) in 2 months or less.
Shape	A consolidation pattern forms after price doubles. It usually doesn't look like a flag or pennant, just a pause in the price rise.
Volume	Recedes for best performance
Confirmation	The pattern confirms as valid when price closes above the highest peak in the pattern, which is usually the flagpole top.

Satish Gaire

Gaps

Gap Type	Discussion
Area, common or pattern gaps	These are synonyms for the same gap type. Occurs in congestion (trendless markets) and closes quickly, usually in a few days. Volume on the gap day may be high but returns to normal in a day or two. Few new highs (upward trends) or lows (downward trends) occur after the gap. A distinctive price curl as the gap closes quickly is a clue to this gap type.
Breakaway gaps	Starts a new trend and the gap often occurs on leaving a consolidation area, usually on high volume on the gap day, which can continue for several days. Price trends for several days.
Continuation, measuring, or runaway gaps	These are synonyms for the same gap type. Gap occurs during a straight-line advance or decline. Price makes new highs or lows without closing the gap. Volume is usually high.
Ex-dividend gaps	Caused by a dividend distribution. Price moves down by the amount of the dividend and a gap appears but it's usually closed by the end of the trading day.
Exhaustion gaps	Happens at the end of a trend on high volume. The gap is usually not followed by new highs or lows, and the gap may be unusually tall. After the gap, price consolidates or reverses direction. Commonly occurs after continuation gaps. Exhaustion gaps usually close within a week.

26 Head-and-Shoulders
Bottoms

Characteristic	Discussion
Price trend	Downward leading to the pattern
Shape	A 3-valley pattern with the middle valley below the others. The pattern should look like an inverted person's head and shoulders, proportional, and not lopsided.
Symmetry	The two shoulders should bottom near the same price, be nearly the same distance from the head, and look similar (both wide or both narrow).
Volume	Highest on the left shoulder or head, diminished on the right shoulder. Trends downward 65% of the time.
Neckline	Joins the two armpits.
Confirmation	The pattern confirms as a valid one when price closes above a down-sloping neckline or above the right armpit when the neckline slopes upward.

Satish Gaire

27 Head-and-Shoulders

Bottoms, Complex

Characteristic	Discussion
Price trend	Downward leading to the pattern.
Shape	A head-and-shoulders bottom with multiple shoulders or multiple heads but rarely both.
Symmetry	The shoulders should bottom near the same price, be nearly the same distance from the head, and look similar to their mirror opposite.
Volume trend	Usually higher on the left side of the pattern. Trends downward 65% of the time.
Neckline	Joins the highest armpits.
Confirmation	The pattern confirms as a valid one when price closes above a down-sloping trendline or above the right armpit when the neckline slopes upward.

Characteristic	Discussion
Price trend	Upward leading to the pattern
Shape	Looks like a head perched atop two shoulders. A three-peak pattern with the middle peak above the others. The pattern should look like a person's head and shoulders, proportional, and not lopsided.
Symmetry	The two shoulders should peak near the same price, be nearly the same distance from the head, and look similar (both wide or both narrow peaks).
Volume	Highest on the left shoulder followed by the head. Trends downward 61% of the time.
Neckline	Joins the two armpits.
Confirmation	The pattern confirms as a valid one when price closes below an up-sloping neckline or below the right armpit when the neckline slopes downward.

29 Head-and-Shoulders

Tops Complex

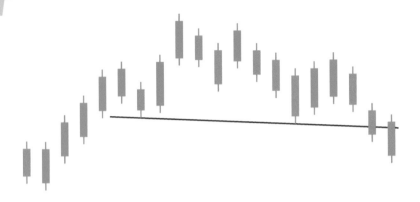

Characteristic	Discussion
Price trend	Upward leading to the pattern.
Shape	A head-and-shoulders top with multiple shoulders or multiple heads, but rarely both.
Symmetry	The shoulders should peak near the same price, be nearly the same distance from the head, and look similar (both wide or both narrow peaks) compared to their mirror opposite.
Volume	Usually higher on the left side of the pattern.
Neckline	Joins the lowest armpits and is often nearly horizontal. Rarely does it slope steeply.
Confirmation	The pattern confirms as valid when price closes below an up-sloping neckline or below the right armpit when the neckline slopes downward.

30

Horn
Bottoms

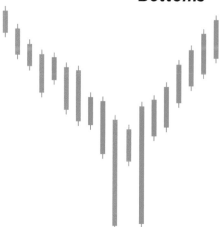

Characteristic	Discussion
Weekly chart	Use the weekly chart to locate horns.
Price trend	Downward leading to the pattern.
Shape	Looks like an inverted steer's horn, two parallel price spikes separated by a week.
Spikes	The spikes should be longer than most in the past year, but in the updated statistics, I didn't concern myself with spike length and performance improved... They should plummet below the surrounding price landscape, including the middle week.
Confirmation	The pattern confirms as valid when price closes above the highest price in the 3-week pattern.

Satish Gaire

31 Horn
Tops

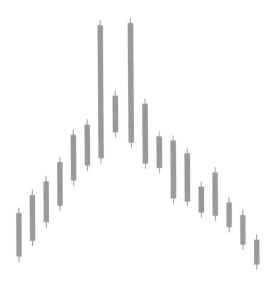

Characteristic	Discussion
Weekly chart	Use the weekly chart to locate horns.
Price trend	Upward leading to the pattern.
Shape	Looks like a steer's horn, two parallel price spikes separated by a week.
Spikes	The spikes should be longer than most in the past year, but be flexible.
Confirmation	The pattern confirms as valid when price closes below the lowest price in the 3-week pattern.

32

Island Reversals
Bottoms

Characteristic	Discussion
Price trend	Tops have price trending upward to the island; bottoms have price trending downward.
Shape	Gaps separate a price island from the mainland.
Gaps	Two gaps must share some or all of the same price.
Volume	High on the day price makes the second gap.
Duration	The island can be one day to several months long.

Satish Gaire

33 Island Reversals

Tops

Characteristic	Discussion
Price trend	Tops have price trending upward to the island; bottoms have price trending downward.
Shape	Gaps separate a price island from the mainland.
Gaps	Two gaps must share some or all of the same price.
Volume	High on the day price makes the second gap.
Duration	The island can be one day to several months long.

34

Island
Long

Characteristic	Discussion
Price trend	Price can trend in any direction leading to the island.
Shape	Non-aligned gaps separate a price island from the mainland.
Gaps	Two gaps that setoff the long island do not share the same price.
Wide gaps	Look for gaps at least $1 wide. This is an arbitrary number.
Length	Look for islands shorter than 4 months. This is an arbitrary limit.
Sequence	Islands tend to get shorter as they appear in a price trend. Thus, they can signal a trend change.
Breakout	The day after the second gap is the breakout day.

Satish Gaire

35 Measured Move

Down

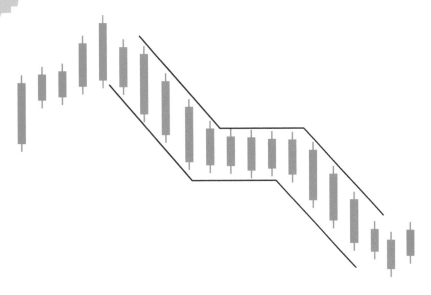

Characteristic	Discussion
Trend	Measured moves (MMDs) are reversal patterns so look for an upward price trend leading to the MMD.
First leg	Any minor high which leads to a minor low.
Corrective phase	The computer algorithm to find these patterns looks for retraces of at least 70%. Those lead to the best measure-rule performance.
Second leg	Price ends the pattern at a minor low.

36 Measured Move

Up

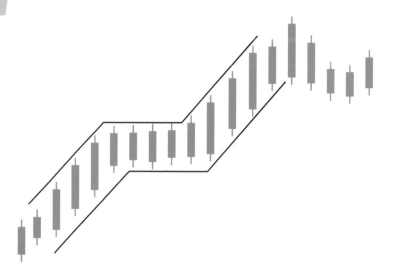

Characteristic	Discussion
Trend	Measured moves are reversal patterns so look for a downward price trend leading to the start of the measured move (for the best performance).
First leg	Any minor low which leads to a minor high.
Corrective phase	The computer algorithm looks for retraces of at least 70%. Those lead to the best measure-rule performance.
Second leg	Price ends the pattern at a minor high.

Satish Gaire

37 One-Day Reversals
Bottoms

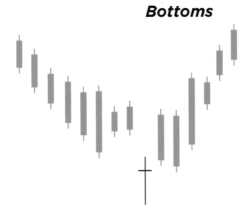

Characteristic	Discussion
3 bars	The pattern is composed of one bar, but for identification, I use three bars, one day before to one day after the one-day reversal.
Bottom	Look for the pattern in a short-term down trend. In other words, wait for an upward breakout (a close above the top of the pattern).
Open and close	The open and close on the one-day reversal must be within 25% of the intraday high.
Surrounding days	The low price of the two adjacent bars must be above the mid point of the one-day reversal. This should make the one-day reversal bar stand alone, like a tree atop a peak (only inverted).
Tall	The one-day reversal should be at least as tall as the one-month average height of other price bars.
Volume	High volume should be present on the one-day reversal. However, I excluded this requirement since the pattern is rare enough without it.

38 One-Day Reversals

Tops

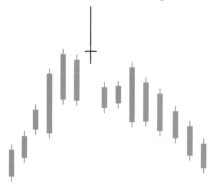

Characteristic	Discussion
3 bars	The pattern is composed of one bar, but for identification, I use three bars, one day before to one day after the one-day reversal.
Top	Look for the pattern in a short-term up trend. In other words, wait for a downward breakout (a close below the bottom of the pattern).
Open and close	The open and close on the one-day reversal must be within 25% of the intraday low.
Surrounding days	The high price of the two adjacent bars must be below the mid point of the one-day reversal. This should make the one-day reversal bar stand alone, like a tree atop a peak.
Tall	The one-day reversal should be at least as tall as the one-month average height of other price bars.
Volume	High volume should be present on the one-day reversal. However, I excluded this requirement since the pattern is rare enough without it.

Satish Gaire

Pennants

Characteristic	Discussion
Price trend	Can be any direction leading to the chart pattern.
Shape	Looks like a short symmetrical triangle.
Trendlines	Prices move between two converging trendlines.
3 weeks	Pennants are short, 3 weeks long or less. Patterns longer than that are symmetrical triangles, rising or falling wedges.
Flagpole	The flagpole which leads to the pennant should be unusually steep and last several days.
Volume	Downward trend 86% of the time.
Breakout	Upward 57% of the time.

Pipe
Bottoms

Characteristic	Discussion
Weekly chart	Pipes appear on the daily scale but the ones on the weekly charts perform better. Use the weekly chart.
Price trend	Usually downward leading to the pattern.
Shape	Twin and adjacent downward spikes. On a bar chart, the two price bars look like spikes. On a candlestick chart, the candles can be any shape (from doji to Marubozu). In other words, don't let the term spike mislead you.
Overlap	The 2 weeks often have a large price overlap but need not bottom at the same price. The bottom price variation is 1%.
Volume	Most pipes show above average volume on one or both spikes.
Obvious	The pipe should stand-alone and be obvious on the chart. The spike should clear the surrounding price action.
Downtrends	The best performing pipes appear at the end of downtrends.
Confirmation	The pattern confirms (becomes a valid pattern) when price closes above the highest high in the pattern.

Satish Gaire

Pipe
Tops

Characteristic	Discussion
Weekly chart	Pipes appear on the daily scale but the ones on the weekly charts perform better. Use the weekly chart.
Price trend	Usually upward leading to the pattern.
Shape	Twin and adjacent upward spikes. On a bar chart, the two price bars look like spikes. On a candlestick chart, the candles can be any shape (from doji to Marubozu). In other words, don't let the term spike mislead you.
Spikes	The spikes should be longer than most others in the past year, but be flexible. They should tower over the surrounding price landscape.
Overlap	The spikes should have a large price overlap.
Variation	The price variation between tops is usually small but can vary up to $1 or more for high price stocks. The average difference is 20 cents.
Volume	The right spike has lower volume when compared to the left spike. This is an observation, not an identification requirement.
Obvious	The pipe should stand-alone and be obvious on the chart.
Retrace	The best performing pipes appear at the top of a retrace in a prolonged downtrend.
Confirmation	The pattern confirms when price closes below the lowest price in the pattern.

42

Rectangle
Bottoms

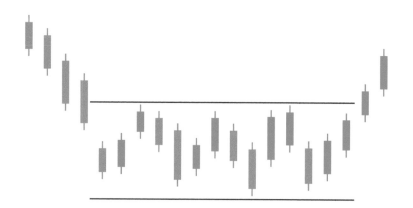

Characteristic	Discussion
Price trend	Downward leading to the chart pattern.
Shape	Prices have flat tops and flat bottoms, crossing the pattern from side to side following two parallel trendlines.
Trendlines	Two near horizontal trendlines bound price action.
Touches	Price should touch one trendline at least three time and the other trendline twice (5-touch minimum) using distinct peaks and valleys.
Volume	Trends downward at least 71% of the time.
Breakout	Upward 59% of the time.

Satish Gaire

43

Rectangle
Tops

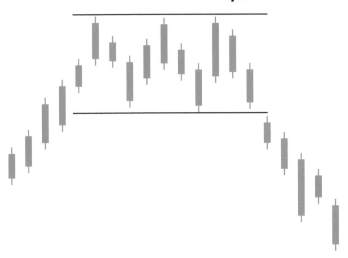

Characteristic	Discussion
Price trend	Upward leading to the chart pattern.
Shape	Prices have flat tops and flat bottoms, crossing the pattern from side to side following two parallel trendlines.
Trendlines	Two near horizontal trendlines bound price action.
Touches	Price should touch one trendline at least three times and twice on the other trendline, using distinct peaks and valleys, but be flexible.
Volume	Trends downward 70% of the time.
Breakout	Upward 63% of the time.

44

Rounding
Bottoms

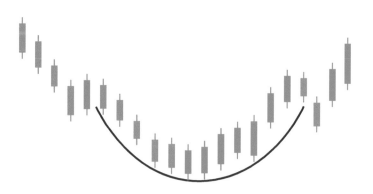

Characteristic	Discussion
Weekly or daily	The pattern appears on either the daily or weekly chart. Concentrate on finding them on the weekly scale because the rounded nature is more apparent.
Price trend	Price trends upward to the pattern 67% of the time (that is, 67% act as continuation patterns).
Shape	Look for a rounded bowl shape, usually over many months and usually after an upward price trend.
Bump	Price may shoot up midway through the turn, near the bottom, but price usually retraces most (not all) of the way back to where it started.
Confirmation	I use a close above the left peak because price on the right might not pause at a minor high.

Satish Gaire

Rounding

Tops

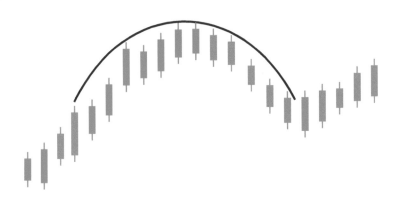

Characteristic	Discussion
Weekly or daily	Rounding tops are large enough to appear on the weekly or daily chart.
Price trend	Upward leading to the chart pattern.
Even ends	The rims of the inverted bowl bottom near the same price, but 58% of the time the end is slightly higher than the start.
Rounded turn	Prices form a gentle curve, a half moon shape.
Breakout	A close above the highest high signals an upward breakout. Downward breakouts are a close below the lower of the two rims (the lowest low in the pattern).

46

Scallops
Ascending

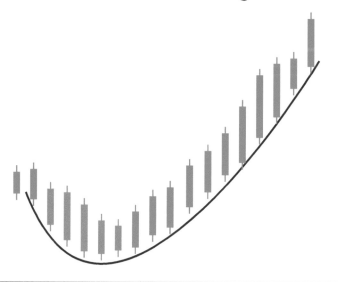

Characteristic	Discussion
Price trend	Upward leading to the chart pattern.
Shape	The chart pattern looks like the letter J. Find two peaks with a rounded valley in between and a higher right peak.
Narrowing	Scallops tend to be wider near the start of a price trend than near the end.
Breakout, confirmation	A close above the highest high signals an upward breakout. Downward breakouts are a close below the pattern's low. A breakout confirms the scallop as a valid chart pattern.

Satish Gaire

Scallops

Ascending and Inverted

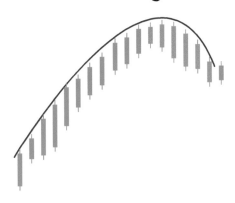

Characteristic	Discussion
Price trend	Most often you'll see these in an upward trend leading to the pattern or at the bullish turning point of a downward price trend.
Shape	Inverted and backward J shape. It looks like the right half of an umbrella. The rise should be a straight, or nearly straight run up, then rounded at the top followed by a small decline.
Smooth top	The peaks should form a rounded turn but larger patterns may not be as smooth.
Retrace	The end of the pattern on the right usually retraces 54% of the prior up move. Avoid 100% retraces.
Volume	Trends downward 70% of the time
Confirmation	The pattern confirms when price closes above the highest high in the pattern.

48

Scallops
Descending

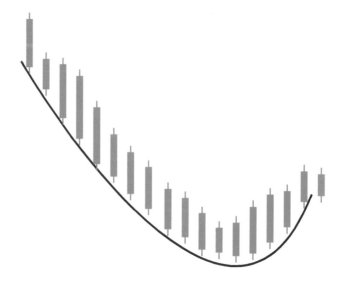

Characteristic	Discussion
Price trend	Usually downward leading to the descending scallop but you'll see them in retraces of an uptrend, too.
Shape	The descending scallop looks like the backward letter J. Find two peaks with a rounded valley in between and the left peak higher than the right one.
Breakout, confirmation	A close above the top of the chart pattern (it used to be the right lip) or below the lowest valley (downward breakout) signals a breakout, confirming the pattern as a valid one.

Satish Gaire

Scallops
Descending and Inverted

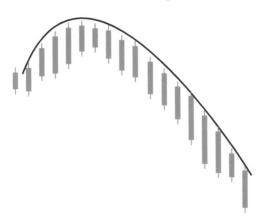

Characteristic	Discussion
Price trend	Usually downward leading to the scallop or at bearish turning points.
Shape	Looks line an inverted J.
Smooth top	Look for a rounded top, not V-shaped, but be flexible.
Down move	From the start of the pattern (point A in the above chart) to its high (B) averages 56% of the following down move from highest peak (B) to scallop end (C, the lowest valley).
Ends	Both the scallop start and end should form at price turning points.
Proportion	The height and width of the scallop should look proportional.
Confirmation	The scallop confirms as valid when price closes below the lowest valley in the pattern without first closing above the scallop's peak.

50 Shark

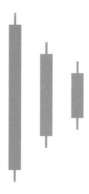

Characteristic	Discussion
Price trend	There is no requirement of a price trend leading to the shark. However, the trend is upward 52% of the time.
3 days	The shark-32 pattern is a three bar pattern.
Shape	Look for two consecutively lower highs and higher lows. If you know what an inside day is, then you're looking for two consecutive ones.
Last Bar	The last bar cannot have the high price equal to the low price. In other words, it cannot be a four price doji (open = high = low = close price).

Satish Gaire

51 Three Falling Peaks

Characteristic	Discussion
Price trend	Upward leading to the pattern then price trends downward.
Shape	Three peaks, each one lower than the prior one.
Symmetry	Each peak should look similar to the others. If you select wide, thick peaks, they should all look that way. The peaks do NOT have to follow a trendline.
Confirmation	The pattern confirms as valid when price closes below the lowest valley in the pattern.

52 Three Rising Valleys

Characteristic	Discussion
Weekly or daily	The pattern appears on either the daily or weekly chart.
Price trend	Usually upward leading to the pattern.
Shape	Look for three valleys -- the bottom of each valley must be above the prior one.
Proportional	Each valley should look similar. Select all narrow ones or all wide ones, all short, or all tall. Don't mix them.
Volume	Trends downward 64% of the time.
Confirmation	The pattern confirms when price closes above the highest peak the pattern.

Satish Gaire

53

Triangles
Ascending

Characteristic	Discussion
Price trend	Can be any direction leading to the chart pattern.
Shape	Triangular. Prices move between two converging trendlines.
Trendlines	Two trendlines bound prices; the top trendline is horizontal and the bottom one slopes upward.
Crossing	Price must cross the pattern from side to side, filling the triangle with price movement, not white space.
Touches	Price must touch one trendline at least three times, the other at least twice, forming distinct valleys and peaks.
Volume	Trends downward at least 78% of the time.
Breakout	Upward 63% of the time and 64% of the way to the triangle apex (for both breakout directions).

54 Triangles

Descending

Characteristic	Discussion
Price trend	Can be any direction leading to the pattern.
Shape	A price pattern bounded by two trendlines, the bottom one horizontal and the top sloping downward.
Touches	Price should touch one trendline at least three times and the other trendline at least twice as distinct peaks or valleys.
Crossing	This is important: Price must cross the pattern from trendline to trendline, nearly filling the available space. Avoid descending triangles with abundant white space.
Volume	Recedes 78% of the time and gets quite low just before the breakout.
Breakout	Can be in any direction but is upward 53% of the time.
Confirmation	The pattern confirms as a valid one when price closes outside one of the trendlines.

Satish Gaire

Triangles
Symmetrical

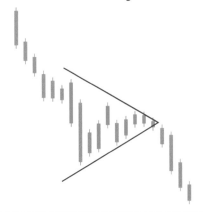

Characteristic	Discussion
Price trend	Can be any direction leading to the chart pattern.
Shape	Triangular. Prices move between two converging trendlines.
Trendlines	Two trendlines bound prices; the bottom trendline slopes up and the top one slopes down.
Crossing	Price must cross the pattern from side to side, filling the triangle with price movement, not white space.
Touches	Price must touch one trendline at least three times and the other trendline at least twice, forming distinct valleys and peaks.
Volume	Trends downward 84% to 86% of the time.
Breakout	Upward 60% of the time and 74% of the way to the triangle apex (for both breakout directions).

Triple
Bottoms

Characteristic	Discussion
Price trend	Downward leading to the pattern but should not drop below the first bottom.
Shape	Three distinct valleys that look similar.
Bottom price	The price variation between bottoms is small such that it appears the three valleys bottom near the same price. Allow variations.
Confirmation	The pattern confirms as a true triple bottom once price closes above the highest peak between the valleys.
Volume	Usually higher on the first bottom than on the last, trending downward 61% of the time, but it may peak beneath each valley.

Satish Gaire

Triple
Tops

Characteristic	Discussion
Price trend	Upward leading to the pattern.
Shape	Three peaks near the same price with a downward breakout.
Middle peak	Sometimes the middle peak is priced marginally below the other two.
Volume	Trends downward 62% of the time, but is usually high beneath formation of each peak.
Bear market	More triple tops appear in bear markets than in bull markets.
Confirmation	The pattern becomes valid when price closes below the lowest valley in the pattern.

58

Wedges
Falling

Characteristic	Discussion
Price trend	Can be any direction leading to the pattern.
Shape	Price follows two down-sloping and converging trendlines.
Touches	Price should touch each trendline at least five times to outline a good pattern. That's 3 touches of one trendline and 2 of the opposite.
Duration	3 weeks is the minimum duration, otherwise it's a pennant.
Volume	Trends downward 72% to 75% of the time until the breakout.
Breakout	Can be in any direction but is upward 68% of the time.
Confirmation	The pattern confirms as a valid one when price closes outside one of the trendlines

Satish Gaire

59

Wedges
Rising

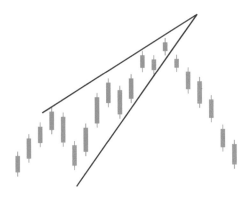

Characteristic	Discussion
Price trend	Can be any direction leading to the pattern.
Shape	A narrowing and rising triangle shape.
Trendlines	Price bounces between two up-sloping and converging trendlines.
Touches	Price should touch (at a minor high or minor low) each trendline at least five times to outline a good pattern. That's 3 touches of one trendline and 2 of the opposite.
Duration	3 weeks is the minimum duration, otherwise it's a pennant.
Volume	Trends downward 79% of the time until the breakout.
Breakout	Can be in any direction but is downward 60% of the time.
Confirmation	The pattern confirms as a valid one when price closes outside one of the trendlines.

Weekly Reversals
Downside

Characteristic	Discussion
Weekly data	Look for downside weekly reversals using weekly data (weekly scale) on the chart.
Price trend	Prices should be trending up leading to the pattern.
2 weeks	Downside weekly reversals are a two-bar pattern.
Shape	On the second bar of the pattern, look for a higher high and lower low (an outside week). The price bar spans beyond the prior week's range.
Lower close	The last bar must close below the prior bar's low.

Satish Gaire

Weekly Reversals
Upside

Characteristic	Discussion
Weekly data	Look for upside weekly reversals using weekly data (weekly scale) on the chart.
Price trend	Prices should be trending down leading to the pattern.
2 weeks	Upside weekly reversals are a two-bar pattern.
Shape	On the second bar of the pattern, look for a higher high and lower low (an outside week). The price bar spans beyond the prior week's range.
Higher close	The last bar must close above the prior bar's high.

Bonus Offer

You can get all these charts on the go your from
TradingUniversity.io
Use Code: FRCM35 for 100% Discount

Follow Satish Gaire At

- @sgaire
- @gairesatish
- SatishGaire.com
- TradingUniversity.io
- EvilTrader.net

CPSIA information can be obtained
at www.ICGtesting.com
Printed in the USA
BVHW021150100121
597490BV00001B/8